# Drawing Frogs
## Volume 2
# How to Draw Frogs
# For the Beginner

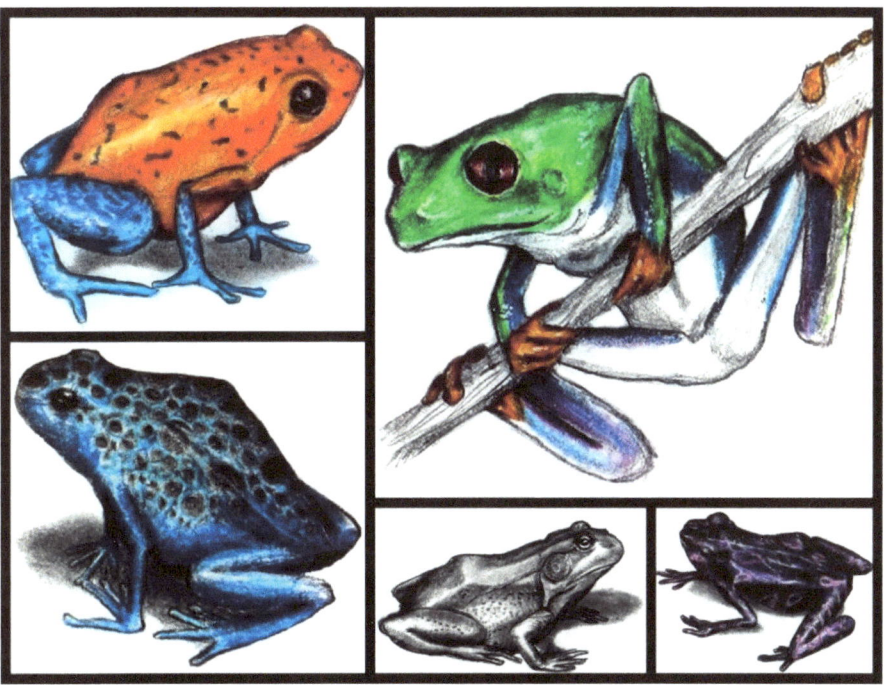

## Learn to Draw Series
Adrian Sanqui

## Mendon Cottage Books

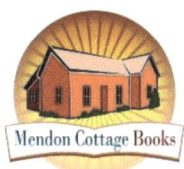

*JD-Biz Publishing*

Learn How to Draw Books for the Absolute Beginner

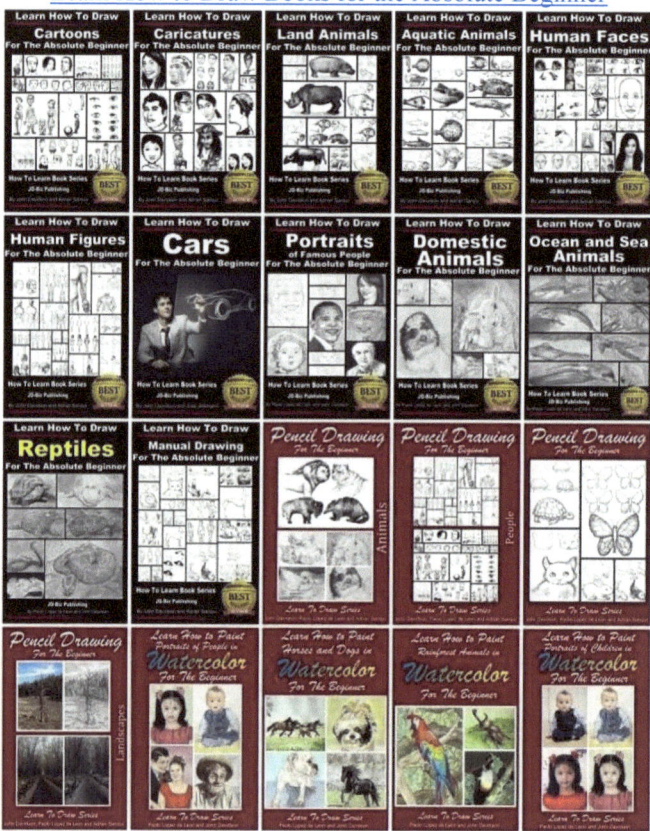

# Table of Contents

# Drawing tools

## Pencils

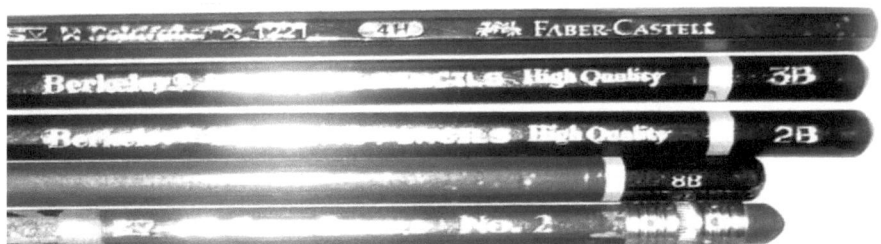

The most important tool you need to be able to enhance your drawing skills is a medium that can be corrected if you made some sloppy line strokes. Knowing and using more than just one type of pencil is a big help and it is better if you have pencils of different grades so you can easily produce the kind of lightness or darkness you want to make. The 'H' engraved near the pencil's tip (side of eraser) stands for "hardness" and it ranges from 2H to 9H. A pencil with only an "H" mark and doesn't have a number means 1H. The most common type (the one available anywhere) of pencil that does not indicate its grade mark is usually a 2H pencil. The "B" marking of pencils stand for "blackness", this means that they can easily produce darker line marks and are softer than H pencils. It ranges from HB (hard and dark) to 9B (very soft and very dark), so when it comes to B pencils, the higher the number is; the softer and darker it becomes. Different brands have different softness, hardness and blackness levels, so if you are going to use a certain brand for the first time, you should try them out first before applying it on your main drawing.

# Charcoal pencils

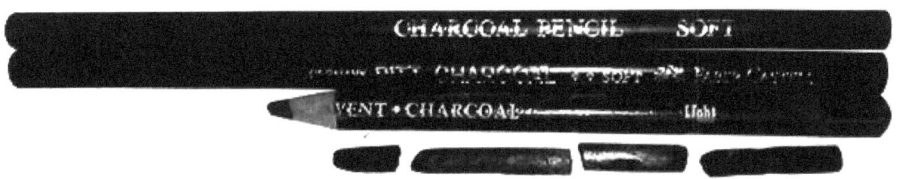

Charcoal pencils also come in different grades. The generic grades of soft, medium and hard are available in different brands. Charcoal pencils are a bit messy to work with; even the 'hard' grade charcoal pencil is still relatively softer compared to those with 4B to 6B grade pencils. It is most advisable for drawings that would require a lot of smeared shading for a smoother and wider portrayal of gradation.

# Mechanical pencil

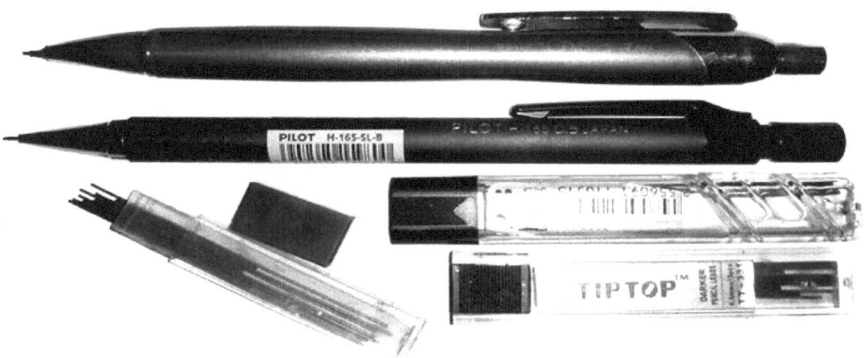

A mechanical pencil has a consistent wick or point which makes it easier for you to maintain the thickness of the line marks you produce. Mechanical pencils are good for small and subtle detailing that requires very thin lines, instead of sharpening your pencil several times just to have a thin and constant fine point that you need. Different grades of lead or graphite is also available for refilling your mechanical pencil, just make sure that the size of the point your pencil has is also the same as the pencil leads you refill it with. They come in several sizes and style, but what really matters is it does what it's supposed to.

## Sharpener

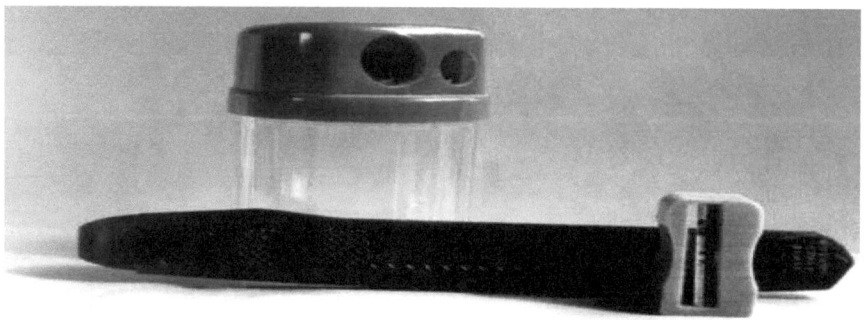

A regular sharpener is quite dependable if you are using H and low B pencils, but if you are going to use it to sharpen a pencil with very soft graphite cores then it may keep on breaking, most especially if you will use it for a charcoal lead pencil. A good substitute for regular sharpeners is a cutter, so you can easily control the pressure that should just be enough to expose the core and achieve a fine point. Cutters are often used if you want a "chisel" point pencil that is very helpful for thick and thin linings.

## Erasers

Pencils are no good if you don't have a good quality eraser, having an eraser is essential if you are going to use a pencil for drawing. Choose a rubber eraser that is soft and not the ones that leave a faint color or worst is a scratch on the paper.

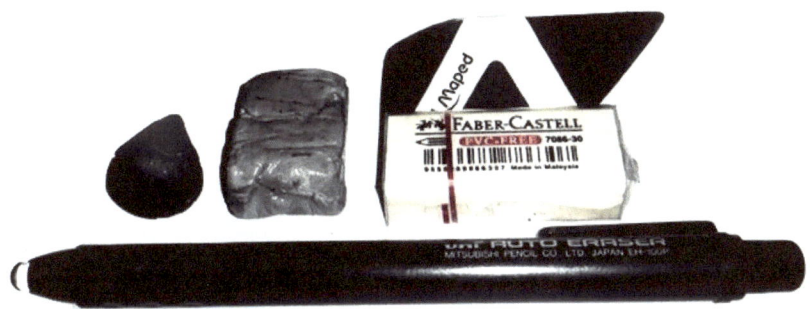

Don't leave your eraser lying around on the table or just anywhere, keep it on a pencil case or anything that can protect it from being exposed on air for too long because some erasers (cheaper ones) harden when it's left lying around because it will dry out and harden.

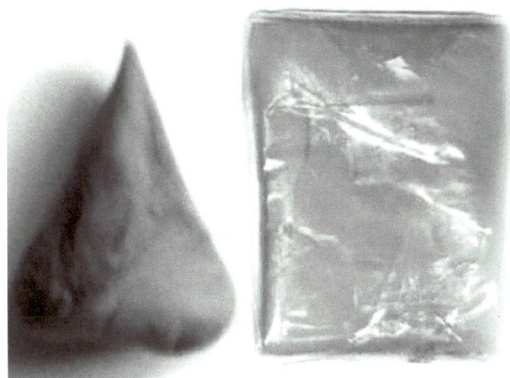

A kneadable eraser is very helpful for making highlights and reaching hardly accessible areas such as the gloss on the eyes or light portions of fingernails and such. It usually looks like a gray slab or a small bar of clay that can be molded or deformed to any shape you desire. It doesn't rub off the marking like usual erasers, but instead, it lifts off the graphite from the paper, like absorbing it. Instead of rubbing the eraser with a certain pressure to remove a marking, carefully dab on the portions you want to erase or to simply decrease the applied graphite or charcoal until you recover the brightness (whiteness of the paper) you want. Kneaded erasers can still be useful as long as they aren't already too dirty or dry. Keep it in a concealed container to lengthen its usefulness, because just like how good it is for absorbing graphite, it would also easily catch dust.

## Smudge sticks

A smudge stick is used for smearing the shades on the portions that are hard to access. Some artists dull down the other tip so it can be used for distributing the shades on the big areas. To avoid ruining the smudge stick, use a sand paper to make a blunter tip or to make it even pointier. Smudge sticks or blending stumps comes in different sizes, choose what best fits your needs and it will be a big help for blending gradations. Smudge sticks are cheap and are available on art stores. Common smudge sticks are just rolled and compressed hard papers, so try not to get it wet.

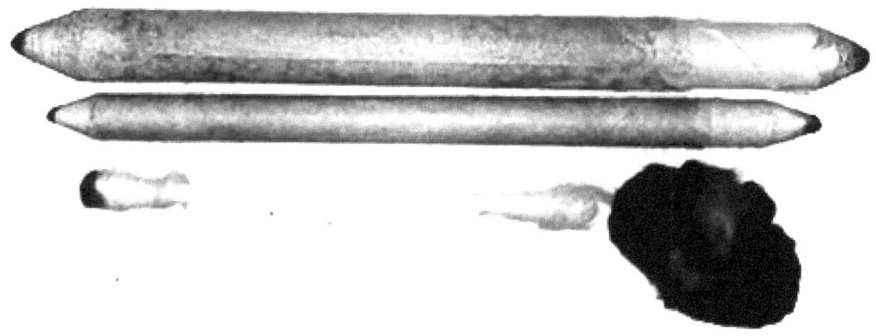

Keep those used up smudge sticks even if it's already in a rugged state (dirty or worn out), you never know when it might get handy. Dirty smudge sticks are useful for producing faint shades, and those with torn up tips can make textures that you might find useful.

If ever you cannot find a smudge stick available (although, I doubt this would be a problem if you have art stores near you, and if not, you can just order online. It is quite cheap) you can just make a tortillion for a temporary smudging tool (some artists actually prefer this one instead of smudge sticks). Use a thick piece of paper (like those on sketch pads, preferably the ones for watercolor drawings. Do not use thin and shiny papers). Fold it on one side and roll it up to create a cone, with the folded side at the tip.

## Coloring materials

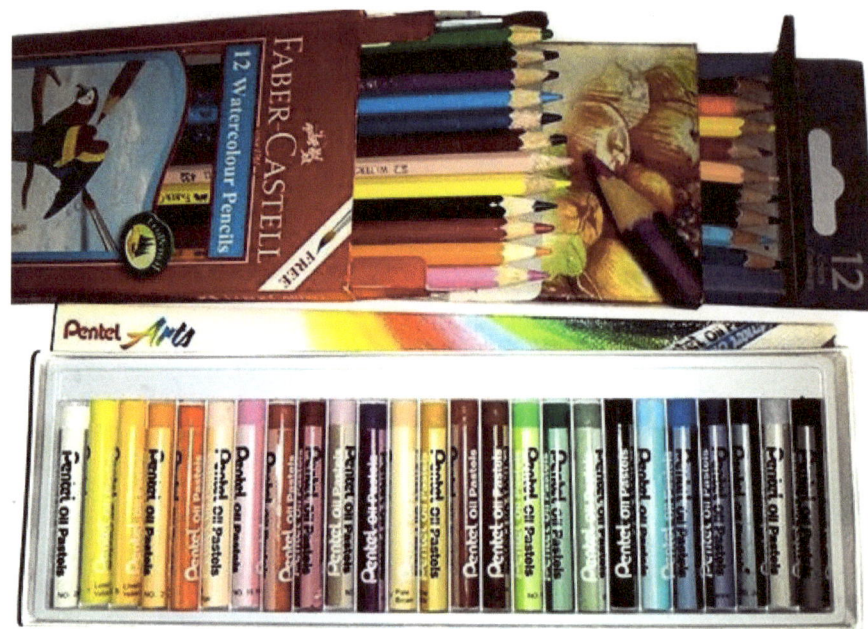

If you are planning to color your drawing, choose a coloring tool that best fits your needs.

Oil pastels are good for blending and synchronizing different colors together. It might get messy on your first trials (if you don't want to get messy, just place a clean piece of paper for your palm rest, to avoid rubbing your palm against the colored portions of your drawing) but you'll get the hang of it as you use it more often. Oil pastels are good for beginners as a practicing tool for smearing different color values.

Color pencils are the next best thing for filling your drawing with colored hatches (linear shading), or even coloring via scribbling. This coloring tool is best for small-sized illustrations. Although, the peak of the tone values that a common color pencil set can produce are far weaker than the oil pastel's, and it cannot be smeared (but there are available color pencils which can produce strong color tones just like oil pastel's or even acrylic's, but they are quite pricy; like the prisma color pencils). This coloring tool is also a good practicing medium for beginners, and my personal favorite for quick colored sketches or even for illustrations with fairly detailed line work.

# Drawing a Common Frog

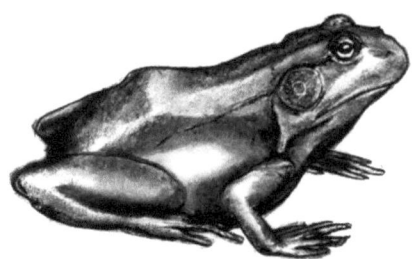

Most of the frogs we see have a shape that is relatively similar to one another; one might have a longer body, other with bigger head or thicker mass, but the primary outline of their basic shape is not far from what we visually perceive as common and how we typically recognize frogs as frogs.

The "bean" or "pear" shaped body combined with short front legs and a longer folded hind legs, usually in a squat position which makes it hard to tell if it is going to jump or just stay put. This idea is going to be your primary basis if you want to draw a simple image of a frog.

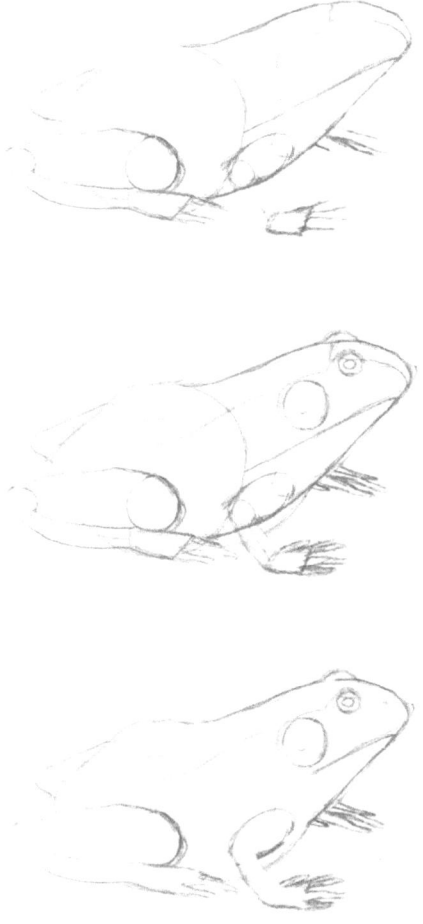

- Draw a basic shape of a pear and use it as a base.

Sketch a sphere to establish the round belly of the frog, and then add an elongated oval to create a base of the frog's body figure.

- Use spheres/circles to easily define the thickness of each leg.

Draw spheres of relative different sizes to approximate mass and length of the limbs. Establish the distance of the joints from the base and use these to define the outlines of each leg.

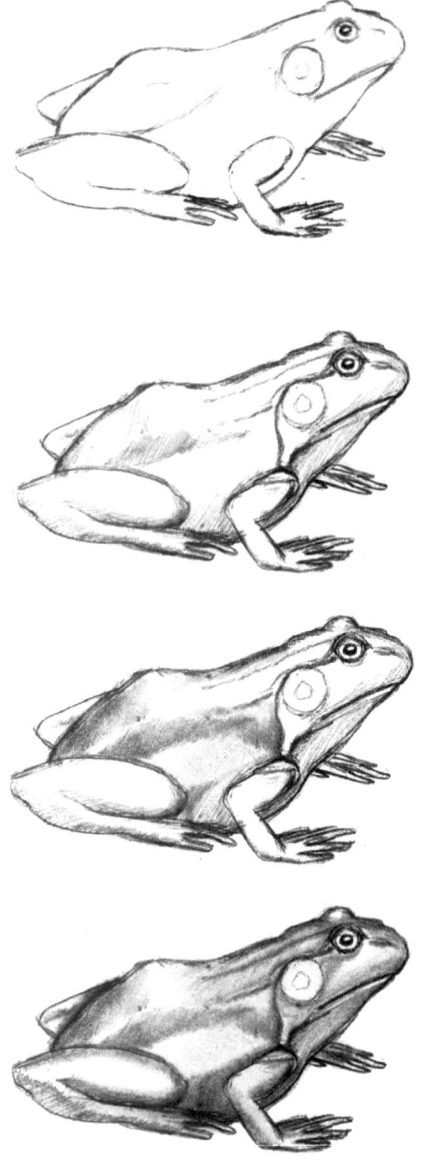

- Use shades to portray the simple dimensions of the body.

Convey the ridges of figure's surface planes by applying shades on the areas that slope inwards.

- Create a skin tone by smearing the shading.

Distribute the shades by pressing lightly to the shades you applied earlier. In this way, the shaded areas will remain as dark-gray and the unshaded areas will have a faint gray tone.

- Elaborate the depiction of the figure's contour dimensions by darkening the farther sides and deeper portions.

Establish the three-dimensional nature of the figure by depicting the farthest portion with the darkest shade and the nearest portion with the lightest shade.

- Finalize the drawing by applying the details of the skin.

Not all frogs have warts on their skin but this one does. The ears may or may not be visible depending on the kind of frog.

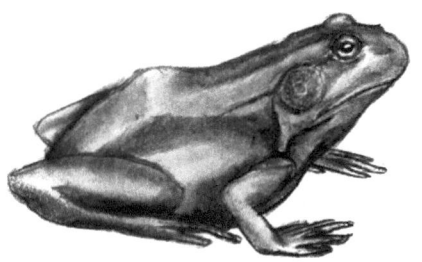

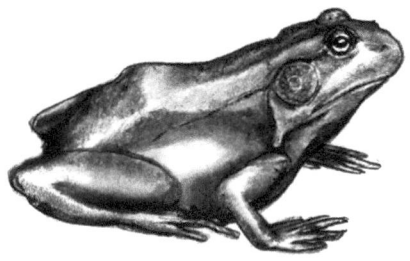

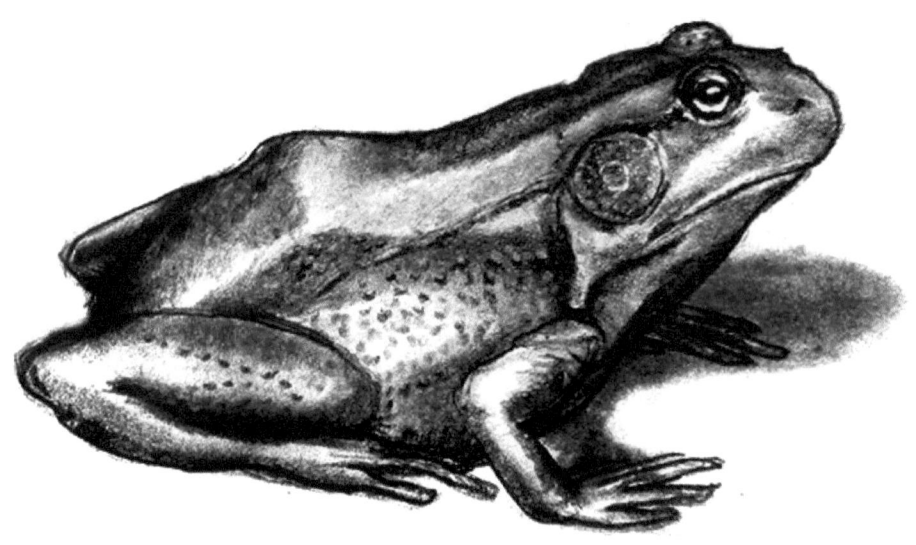

# Common Gestures

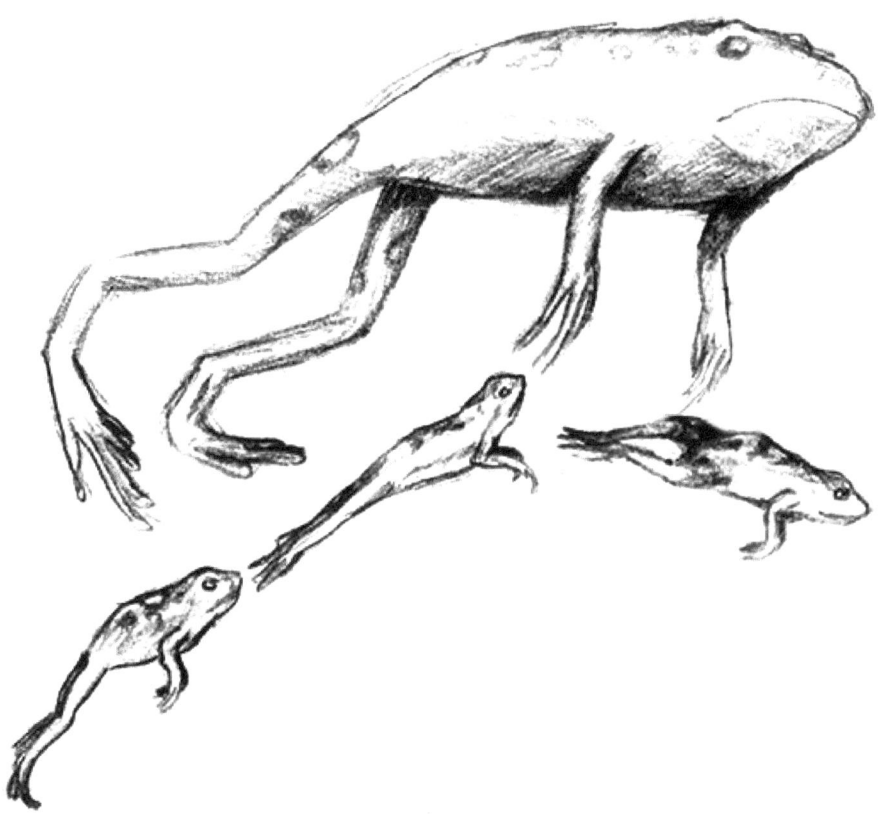

**Hopping**

The difference in length of the fore legs and hind legs becomes apparent when the frog jumps. It would stretch its hind legs widely during and at the moment of leaping, and then quickly reverts to its natural crouching position as it lands.

The base outline (trunk) has no observable changes when a frog leaps/jumps, the head may tilt a little but it depends if either the frog is aiming to relocate on a higher ground/place or it is simply jumping to move further forward.

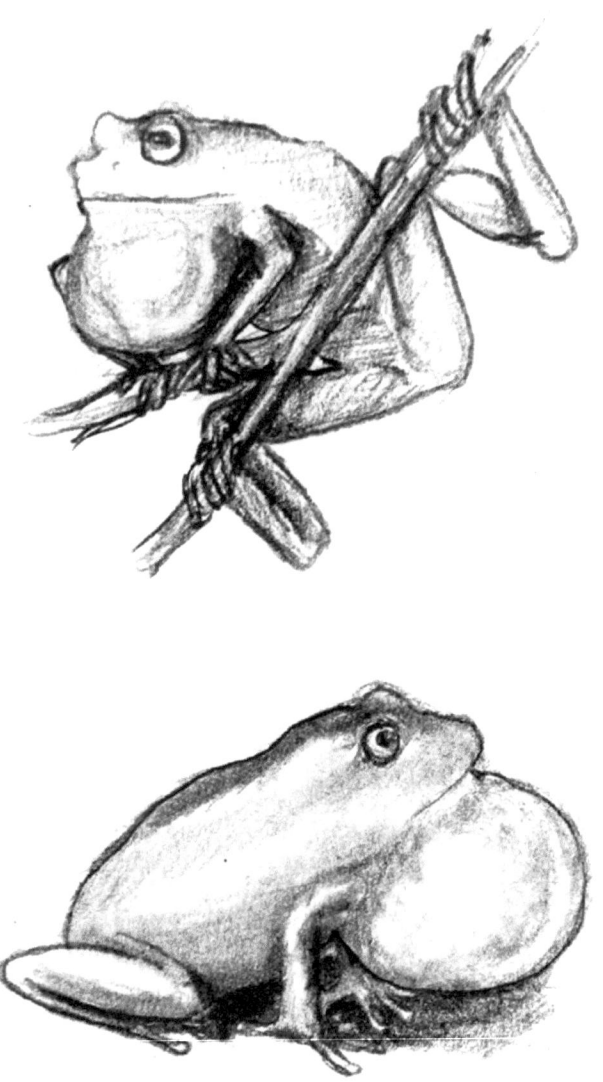

## Croaking

The vocal sacs expands to a size that is relatively bigger than the head of the frog, becoming semi-transparent at the peak of its expansion. Some frogs have two vocal sacs located at the lower side of the head (corners of the mouth). Frogs with single vocal sacs would sit or position in an angle to let their sacs have enough space to stretch upon.

# Purple Fluorescent Frog

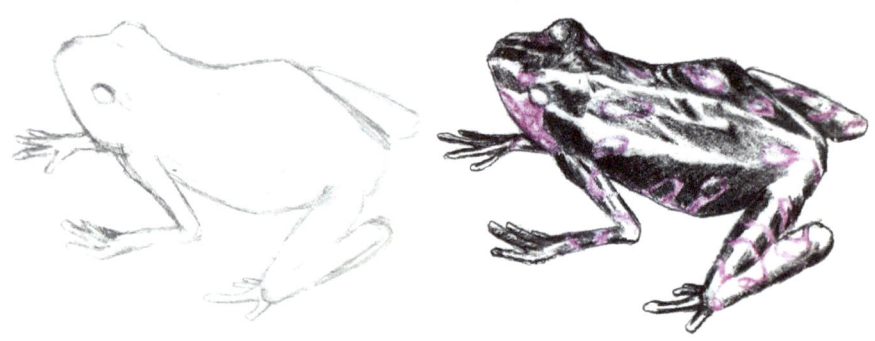

The purple fluorescent frog was accidentally discovered on year 2007, when scientists Paul Ouboter and Mr. Jan Mol was conducting a follow-up survey on the remote wild forest of Nassau Plateau at Suriname in South America. The frog simply outstands from its surroundings due to its dark purplish vibrant color. It belongs to the family of Atelopus, which are also referred as the stub foot or harlequin toads. Atelopus frogs are a big family of toads; many of their species can be cited in Southern and central areas of America. But due to illegal mining and a spreading fungus called the Batrachochytrium dendrobatidis, some of their kinds are extinct, and others endangered, including the purple fluorescent frog. Most Atelopus frogs are diurnal (active during daytime), they are small in size and often bicolored with vibrant hues (having two colors or a color of different values). There is a confusion about this frog's name, the word 'fluorescent' might be describing the frog's vibrant color or (although, no evident proof was ever published or presented) the skin could glow/fluoresce when it is under a black light, since there are other frogs with this characteristic.

It has two colors, or rather, one with two contrasting values. The body is generally purple/brownish-purple with a very dark value, containing irregular markings of bright purple rings. Like most frogs, the body contains a glossy texture. The length and thickness of its body and limbs are common for frogs: with forelimbs being fairly thinner and shorter than the hind limb. In size, the trunk is and head is also regular-shaped, having a fair length and mass. Its eyes and mouth are regular in size, the eyes are dark-colored, and right below it is a dotted band of bright purple, extending down to the forelimbs.

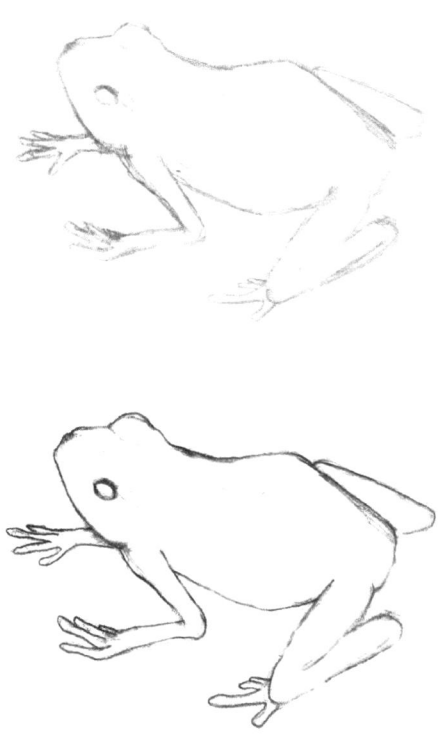

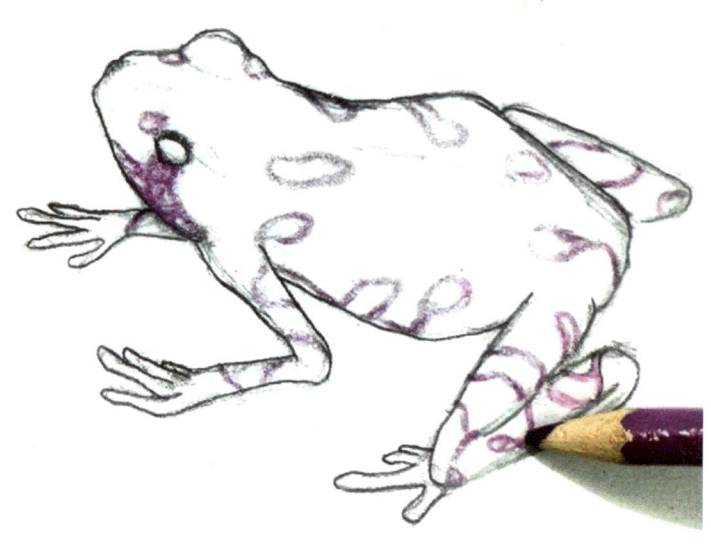

- Establish the main outline of the frog.

Define the contour shape of the frog's figure. Establish the folds of the limbs and see what portions are overlapped. The curves and subtle projections of a frog's body shape outline is well-shown when it is viewed in an upper-side view angle; the robust eyes, the slight protuberance of the lining on the trunk, and the round belly.

When the proportions are properly defined, refine the outlines with smoother and darker lines.

- Define the body markings with purple.

The body of a fluorescent frog is marked with irregular purple rings. The marking are more apparent on the limbs, wrapping each leg and down to the toes. There is also a purple band starting right below the eyes and down to the frog's ventral side. Use a purple (pencil) color directly when establishing the markings, or a violet with a light/bright value.

- Apply some linear shading.

The violet color of the frog's body is dark; in this case, you need to apply a preliminary shading to darken the tone value of the color you are going to apply later.

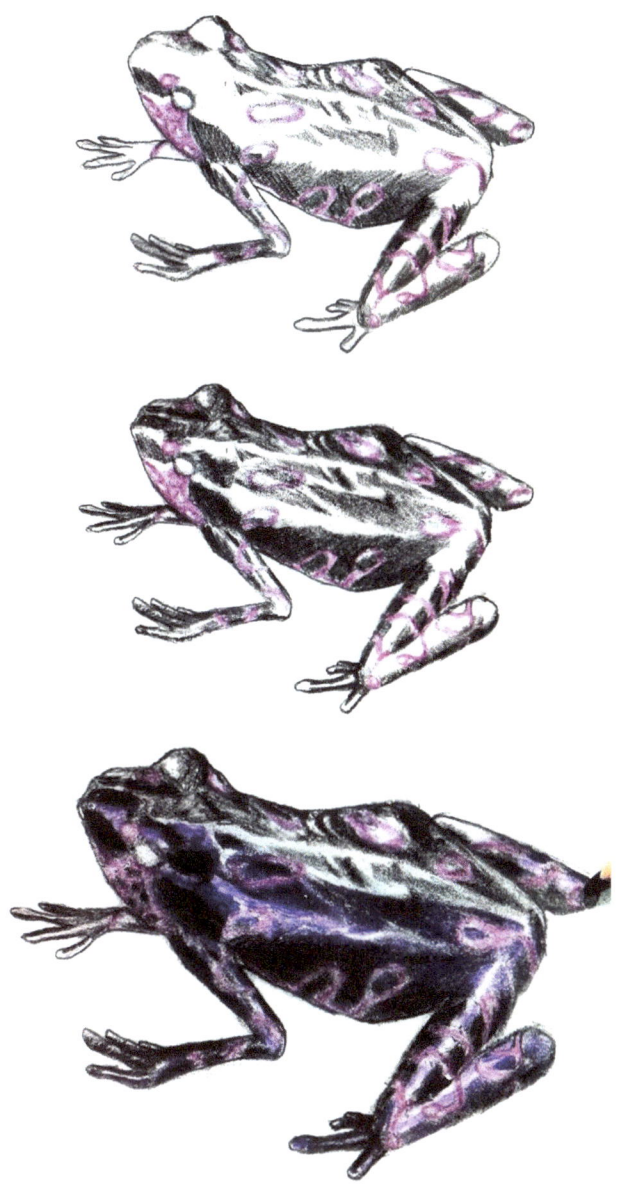

Apply some hatches on the side and at the farther portion of the frog's figure with a dark and fairly thick value. And then apply a lighter shading on the nearer area. Take note of the subtle highlights and the edges at the back of the frog, these unshaded portions establish the slight unevenness of the plane.

For the limbs, only apply shades at the sides. The directions of the hatches you apply are not important, since you will even out this linear shading anyway.

- Smear the shades.

Carefully smudge the linear shades with light scribbling hand strokes. Keep the highlights clean and simply even out the shades to loosen the edges created by the hatches.

- Apply the violet color of the body.

Fill up the areas with the frog's dark violet body color. Control the weight of your hand strokes; the pressure you apply on the (color) pencil depends on the area you are coloring. Use light hand strokes on the edges of the body and the middle area of the legs. Use heavy hand strokes to overlap the darkened areas.

Finalize the drawing by darkening the eyes (take note of the subtle gloss at the center) and cast a shadow. Redefine the main outline and clean up the outer areas.

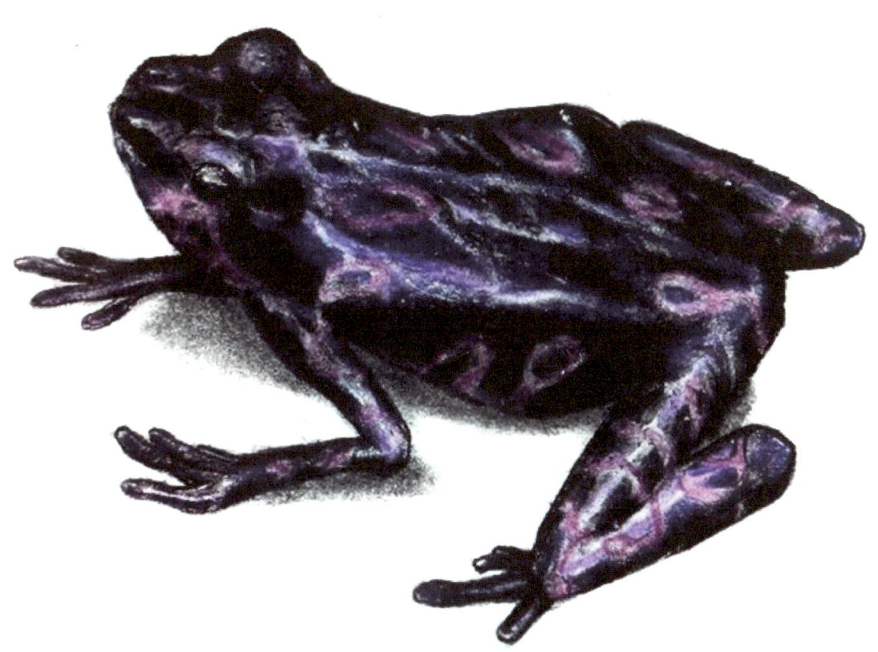

# Red-eyed Tree Frog

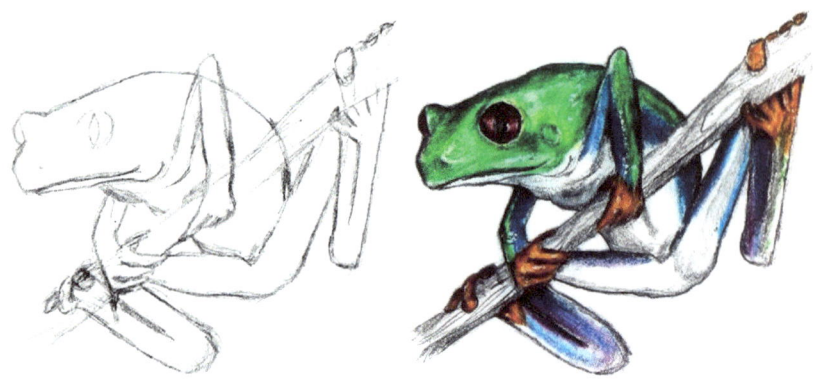

This adorable tree frog is usually being kept as a pet, probably because of its color combination with its big red eyes. The Agalychnis callydrias or commonly referred to as the red-eyed tree frog (although it is not the only frog that is called by this name) is often seen in lowland forests of Mexico, Panama, Costa Rica and Colombia. It is a native inhabitant of the tropical and subtropical forests of South and Central America. As an amphibian that is nocturnal in habit, it can only be seen active at night, hunting for small insects and jumping from tree to tree.

This popular tree frog is known for its vibrant colors. The dorsal side of its body is either bright or dark green, and the ventral side is usually white. The sides of its body contains two colors, a faint purplish blue with thin vertical stripes of yellow. The purplish blue value of the sides of its trunk extends to the undersides of its limbs. Although there are cases which the purple color is not present, and the yellow color extends halfway across the white ventral side of its body.

Its toes are long, fairly thick and ball-pointed having a strong value of orange (Some of its kind has the orange color extending to its limbs instead of the white or purplish-blue color). The fairly slender physique is basically bean-shaped, and the size of the head is fairly proportionate to its body. Its big blood-red eyes has a vertical iris that can be compared to some snakes', they are significantly prominent, bulging from its slender head like it's about to pop off.

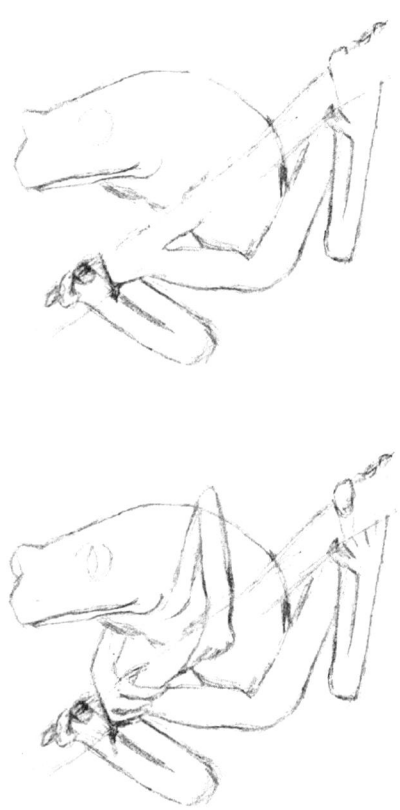

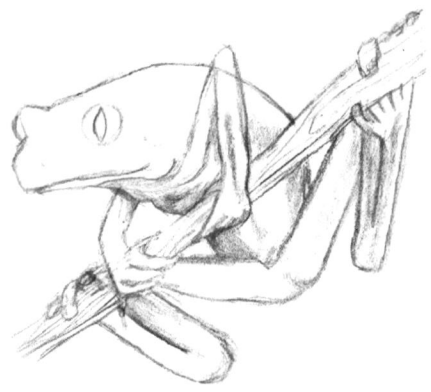

- Establish the primary outline.

A red-eyed tree frog hanging on a branch creates a shape with curvy outline. Use an arc to establish the outline from the head and down to the trunk. The folds of the hind limbs can be easily conveyed with a "W" shape outline, from the frog's bottom and to the toes.

Complete the body outline. Draw the forelimbs and add the frog's features. The eyes of a red-eyed tree frog should be round and very protruding.

- Apply some shades.

Erase any unnecessary sketch lines, overlapped outlines and any excessive line marks. Redefine the main outline of the frog with clean and more visible lines. Apply some shading to establish the contour dimensions of the figure. Shade the side of the trunk, the inner edges and flat planes of the limbs. Also apply a shade on the farther side of the frog's underside.

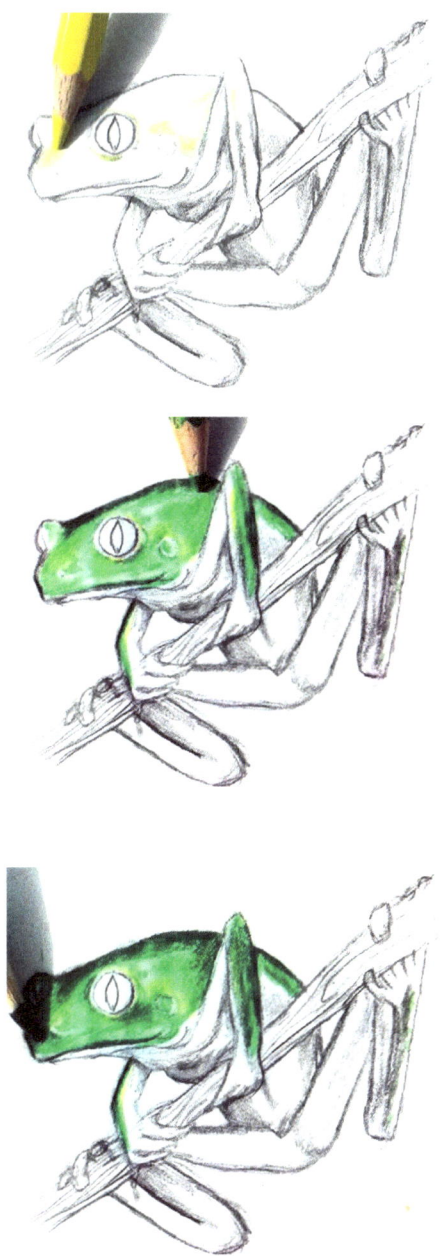

- Apply some yellow color.

Use yellow to create a faint yellowish green value to the bright portions of the frog's body. Apply it on the top plane of the nose, curvy side of the trunk right behind the ears/tympanic membrane, and a ring around the nearer eye. Also apply a lining of yellow on the limbs that should have a bright value.

- Apply the green color of the frog's dorsal side.

To avoid leaving visible line strokes while coloring, use a blunt-point and apply with circular hand strokes.

Fill the dorsal area with green using fairly light hand strokes. Thicken the green by overlapping it with another layer once again. The limbs are green on top with white undersides; apply green color to the dorsal plane of the limbs (the hind limbs will not have any green color because of its position).

Once the green areas are filled, portray the dimensions of the figure by applying a darker green. Overlap/burnish the top plane of the figure, starting from the top of the nose and to the top of the trunk. Also apply a faint dark green on the sides of the trunk and the blunt tip of the nose.

The idea is to create a faint lining and brighter areas from the edge of the nose diminishing down to the nearest side of the trunk. The subtle dark tone of green should also be expressed, like the even plane on the cheek (below the eyes), a faint ring of shadow on the ears, and the inner edges of the green areas on the forelimbs.

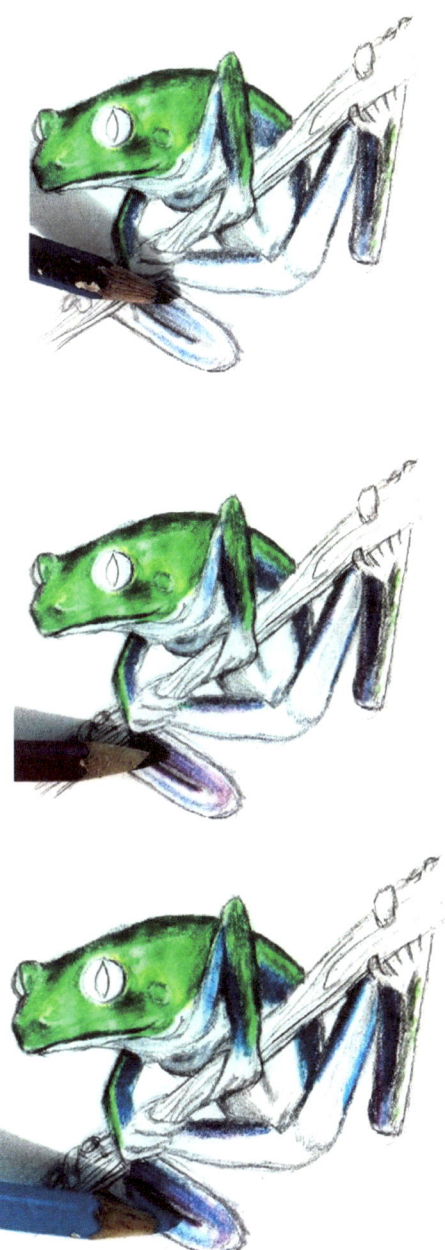

- Apply the blue tone on the sides.

The blue color on the side of the red-eyed tree frog has different tone values; a mixture of dark blue, bluish-purple and blue of a brighter value. To properly convey the mixture of tones, apply the colors with faint circular strokes. The tone becomes very light as it mixes with the white ventral side, adjust the pressure on your hand strokes and make it lighter as you reach the brightest area.

Start with dark blue, fill the blue areas with a loose layer of a sea-blue value.

- Apply some violet color.

Use violet tone as a darker value of dark blue. Apply it on the overlapped areas, the middle of the blue-toned portions on the trunk, and a faint tone on the exposed underside of the hind limbs.

- Burnish the sides with a brighter blue tone.

Overlap the entire blue area with a brighter blue color. The bright sky-blue tone should be the value that mixes up with the other tones of the body, this should be the margin of the blue areas of the frog.

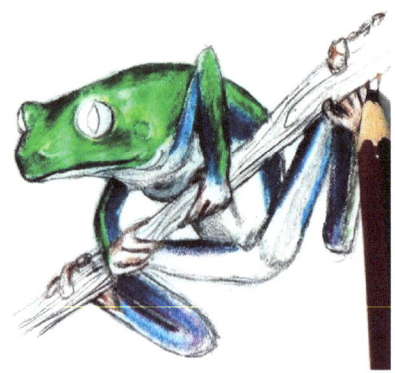

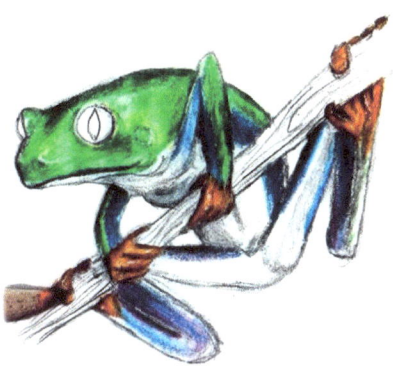

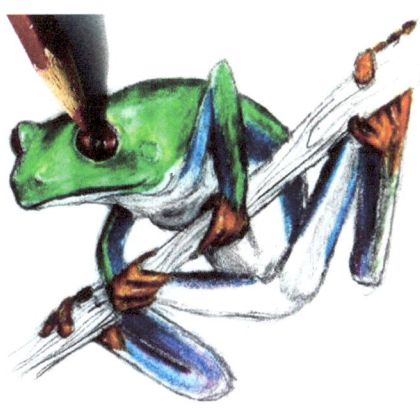

- Color the toes.

Color the inner edges and overlap the inner outlines of the toes with brown, this would be the dark value of orange. And then fill the toes with a strong value of orange.

- Apply the red color of the eyes.

Finalize the coloring by defining the frog's blood-red eye color. Redefine the main outline if necessary, and then apply some subtle highlights.

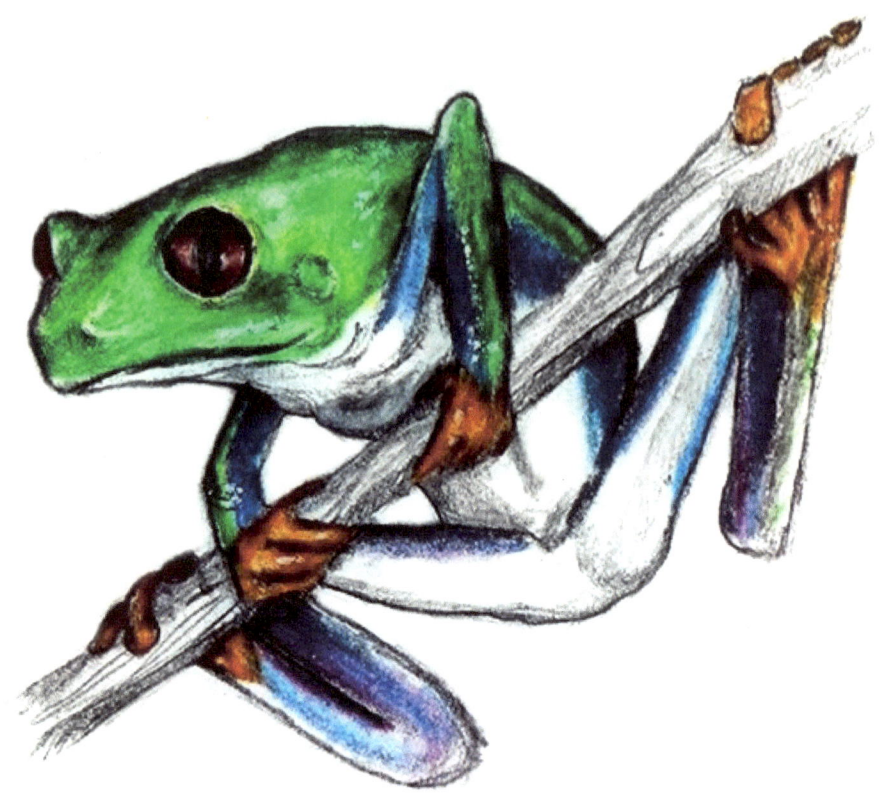

The red-eyed tree frog is a hasty jumper and is quite flexible, hanging on branches in monkey-like positions with the help of its long sticky toes and relatively light body. During the day, it lies motionless on leaves, keeping its flashy colors out of sight: it stays in a tucked position, hiding its strong hued toes and sides by folding its limbs tightly to its body and keeping its toes underneath its trunk, as it effectively blends its green backside to the leaf. But in spite of its clever way of blending, it is often preyed upon by a lot of predators, mostly by birds, lizards, and other bigger forest inhabitants.

# Strawberry Poison Dart Frog

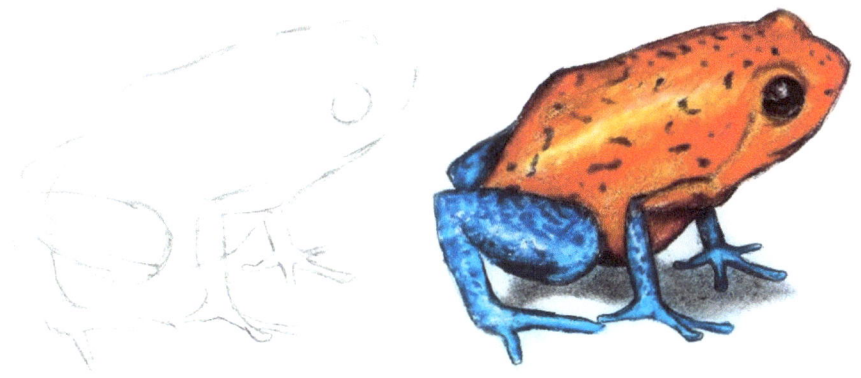

The Oophaga pumilio (formerly referred to as Dendobrates pumilio) or the strawberry poison dart frog (probably due to its bright red color) is a small kind of frog that can be spotted hiding on forest floor, somewhere beneath the bushes and leaf litter. Although it can also be seen amongst the leaves and small puddles (and anywhere that could hold a fair amount of water for their tadpoles. in few cases, even on unnatural litters left on their habitat, like soda cans and such) when hiding and rearing/caring for their young. This frog genus is popular for having more than just few color combinations on their body (the record says it has approximately fifteen to thirty color morphs). It is called the blue-jeans frog because one of the common color morph it is known to; a blue color hind limb on its typical vibrant red body. It is native to South America, and commonly seen on humid lowland forests of northwest of Panama, Nicaragua and Costa Rica. It can grow a length size from seventeen millimeters to an inch. On humid habitats, a male strawberry poison- dart frog makes a distinct sound most of the day to attract females and warn other males to stay away.

Strawberry poison-dart frogs are bicolored. The head and trunk is usually red with different tone value, either blood-red tone or reddish-orange. It is often combined with another contrasting color on its limbs (usually on front toes and the entire hind limbs), such as green, purple or (most common) blue. These secondary coloring could also have a blend of different colors, such as greenish-blue or bluish-purple. It's fairly slender body may or may not contain irregular black spotting around its body. The size and color of the spots may also vary depending on its color morph (like the blue limbs having red or black spots).

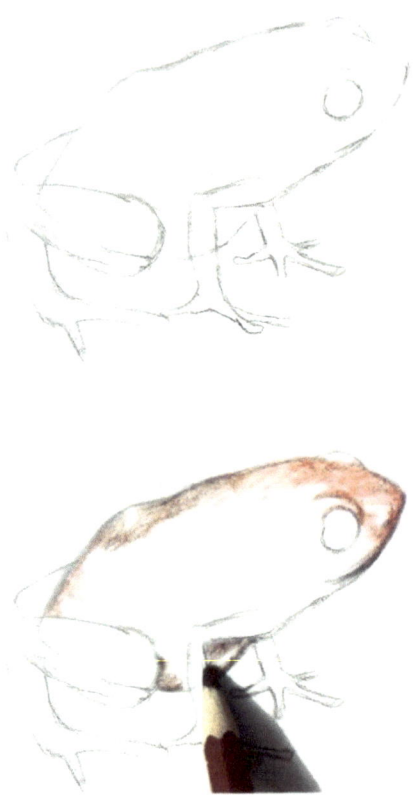

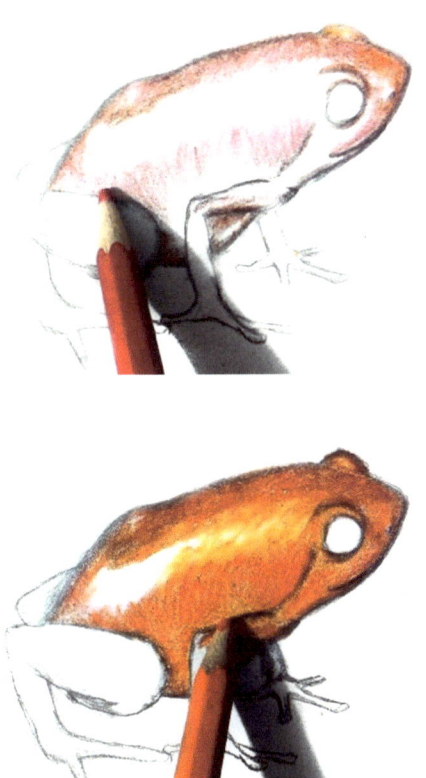

- Draw the main outline.

Establish the size and the position of the frog. The body is almost like bean/leaf-shaped, with the top of the trunk having a subtle protuberance and the belly being round.

- Apply a brown tone in the inner edges.

The color of the frog is basically reddish orange. Combine three values of color to convey a stronger and brighter value of the general skin tone.

Light brown can be used as a darker value of orange, apply it to the inner edges of the main outline and to the farther portions of the figure.

- Apply some red value to the trunk.

Use red as the next stronger value of the reddish orange tone. Apply it to the nearer portion of the trunk and at the gap of the eyes. Overlap the brown color with light and thin strokes of red cross-contour hatches.

- Fill the area of the body with orange.

Overlap the red and brown with orange. Use heavy circular hand strokes and fill up the entire area of the head and the trunk, but leave a lighter tone right above the nearer area of the trunk which you previously colored with red (only color this portion with light strokes to produce s subtle highlight to the body of the frog).

- Re-apply a red color.

Redefine the red tone on the nearer side of the trunk (right below the brightest portion of the body). Simply overlap the orange on this area with another layer of red. Use a blunt tip or the sides of the color pencil with fairly heavy strokes.

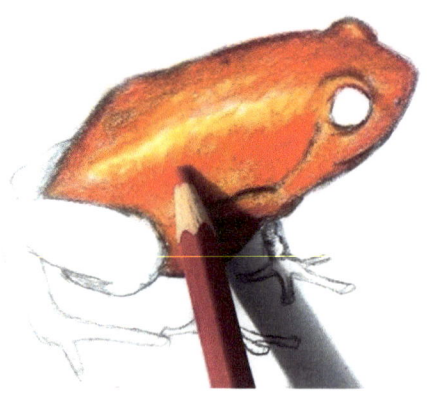

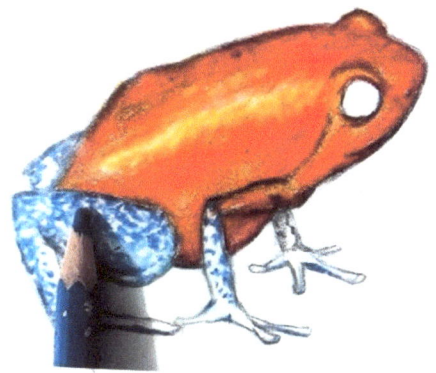

- Fill the limbs with irregular patches of dark blue.

Start defining the color of the legs. It should be blue with irregular markings of a darker blue. Most of the patches should be at the thigh. The color of the forelimbs could be reddish orange (same with the trunk) or blue, and it could also be in half of both colors. The brachium could be reddish orange and the antebrachium could be blue (with few irregular patches). The toes are blue most of the time.

- Burnish the dark blue limbs with a brighter value.

Color the limbs with bright blue. Overlap the dark blue patches and leave a faint highlight at the middle portions of the limbs. Once the blue of a brighter value is applied, make some faint shades of dark blue on inner edges of the legs.

- Define the shade of the eyes.

The darkest shade should be at the center of the iris, and the shade of ring surrounding it should be slightly lighter than the shade on the inner edges of the eyes. Leave a highlight to depict its glossy texture.

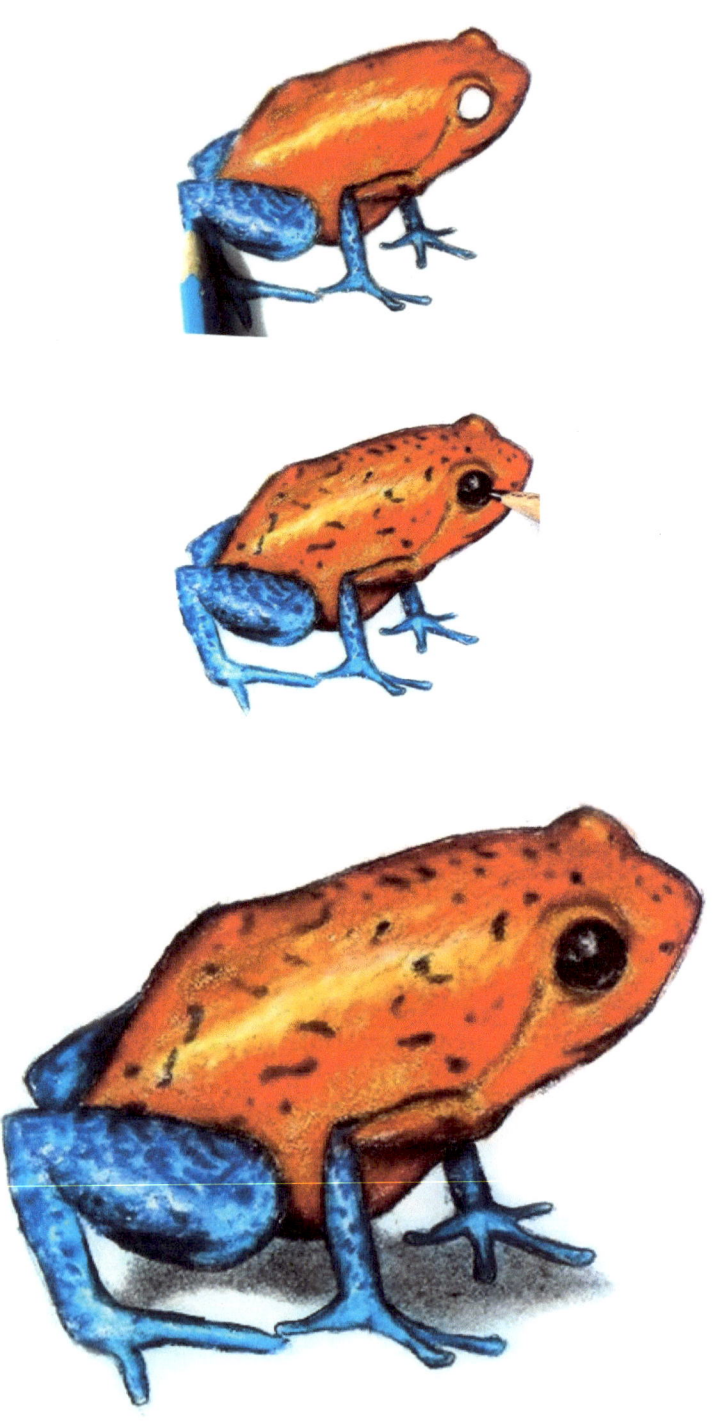

It is also known for its remarkable parenting. the female watches over her tadpoles for   approximately eight weeks, feeding them with her own (unfertilized) egg cells (This habit is vital to their breed, if the tadpole fails to consume its mother's egg cells, it will not have a toxicity level that is enough to obtain the poison it needs to defend itself from any potential predators). And as the mother stays with them, the male waters the nest and ward off the predators (unguarded nests are often attacked by another O. Pomilio, eating the egg cells or bringing them to feed its own tadpoles). When the time is right, the mother relocates each of them to other  watered spots, then visits each of them from time to time (to supply them with her eggs) until they turn into froglets.

# Blue Poison Dart Frog

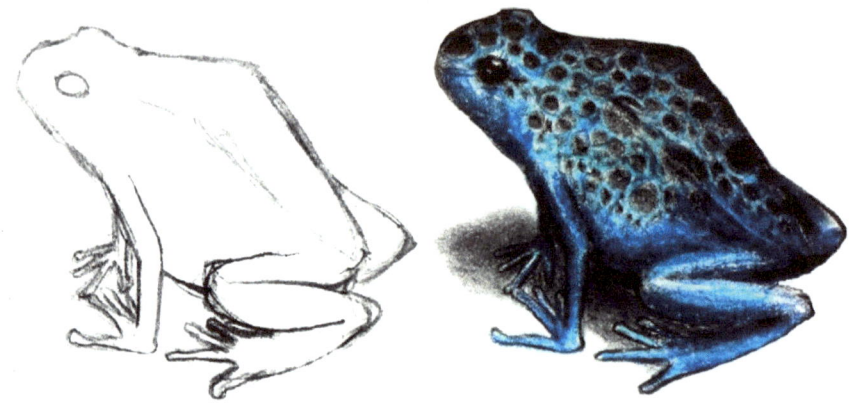

Poison dart frogs are known to have a combination of vibrant colors or a contrasting color value with clearly distinguishable body markings. A strong hued color of their body is an obvious sign or a warning to humans or their predators, that the frog can secrete a certain amount of poison that could either cause skin irritation, a certain kind of intoxicating effect, or even death.

This means that not all poison dart frogs are life-threatening, although it is just safe to try and not aggravate them in any way especially if you do not know much about their specific kind. It is better to just appreciate their beauty with a reasonable distance and give them the respect and privacy they deserve, especially this blue poison that frog which is very territorial.

The blue poison dart frog, also known as Dendobrates tinctorius azureus or the Okapipi (local name) is bigger than the strawberry poison dart frog. It has a body length of three to five centimeters. The shape, or rather, the stance of the Okapipi is crooked (hunchbacked), with its head leveled far from the ground and the back slightly arced.

This poison dart frog is quite protective aside from being aggressive, the poison coating on its skin can paralyze and even kill any predator who makes contact, and it would engage to a fight if its territory is threatened. The spots on their body are never identical, each of them has a unique set of spot marks that serves as their identifier (like a human's fingerprints or the stripes of zebras).

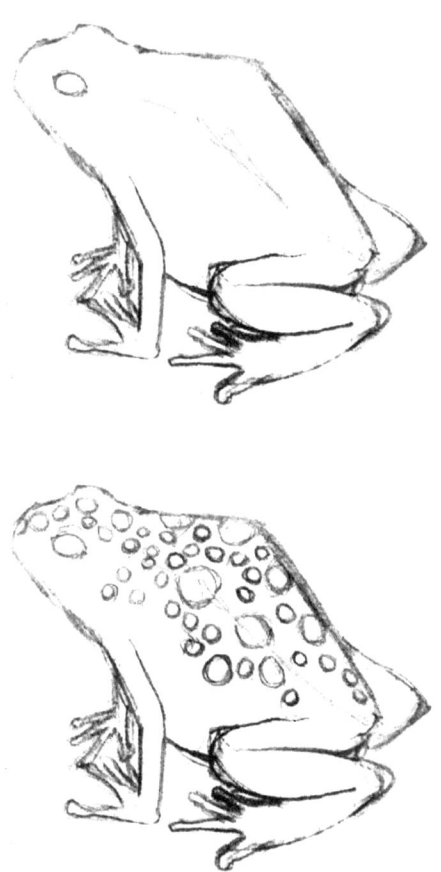

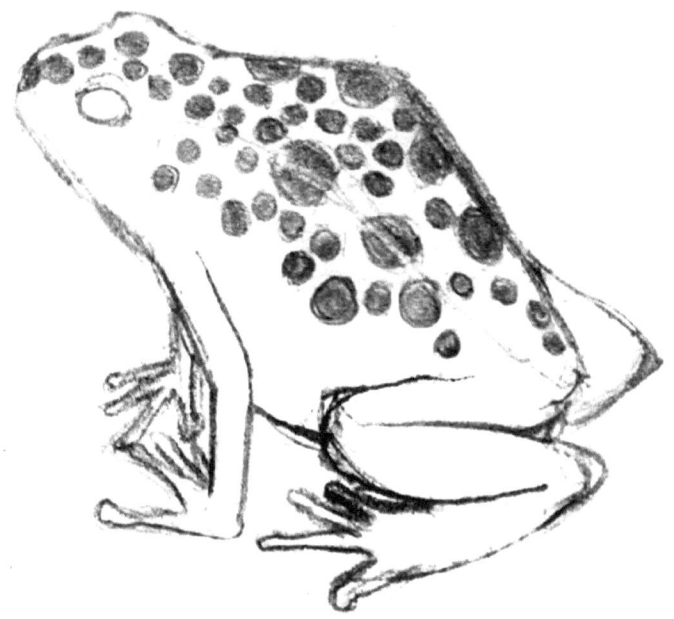

- Sketch the primary outline of the frog.

Convey the basic shape of the frog and establish its size. Remember that this frog has an angular back/trunk because of the way it squats/sits. The forelimbs should be shorter and slimmer that the hind limbs (especially when compared to its thighs).

- Define the spot on the dorsal side of the frog.

Draw the body markings. The sizes the spots are indefinite, covering the dorsal side of the frog from head to trunk and down around the sides.

- Apply some shades.

Make some faint shades on the lower area of the body. Shade the lower curves of the belly (to convey its round shape) and on the lower portion of the head. Also shade the lower sides of the limbs and the overlapped portions (farther legs).

Shade the spots of the body, the tone value depends on the position of the spots (the spots at the back should be darker than the ones at the side) to establish the contour dimensions of the figure.

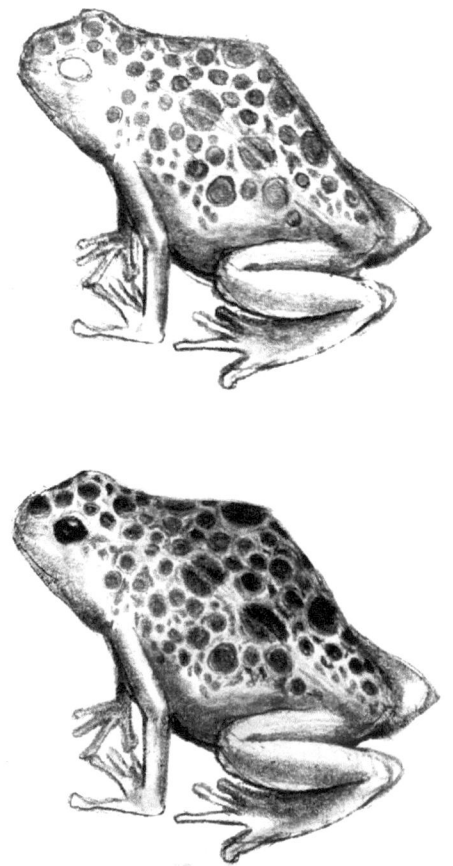

- Elaborate the shading.

Darken the shades of the spots, use heavy scribbling strokes. Shade the eyes with a black colored pencil, the eyes should be darker than the spots. There are subtle shades in between the body marking margining the open spaces.

- Apply a light blue color.

Start coloring the frog. Apply a light blue color to the body. Avoid overlapping the spots and just color the small spaces in-between.

- Apply another blue of a darker value.

Overlap the bright blue with another blue of a darker value. The pressure you put on the strokes depends on the area you are coloring, the lower side/belly of the frog should be darker compared to the mid-portion. The spots should have rings of bright blue. Again, avoid overlapping the spots, these should remain black.

- Darken the areas that should appear darker.

Finalize the drawing by re-shading the strong tones (dark blue value of the darker areas, shades on the overlapped portions, and the farther side of the body). Re-define the main outline and cast a shadow.

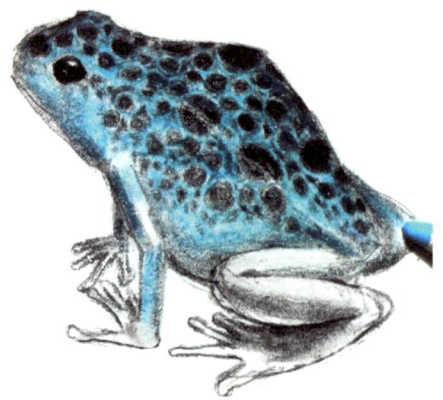

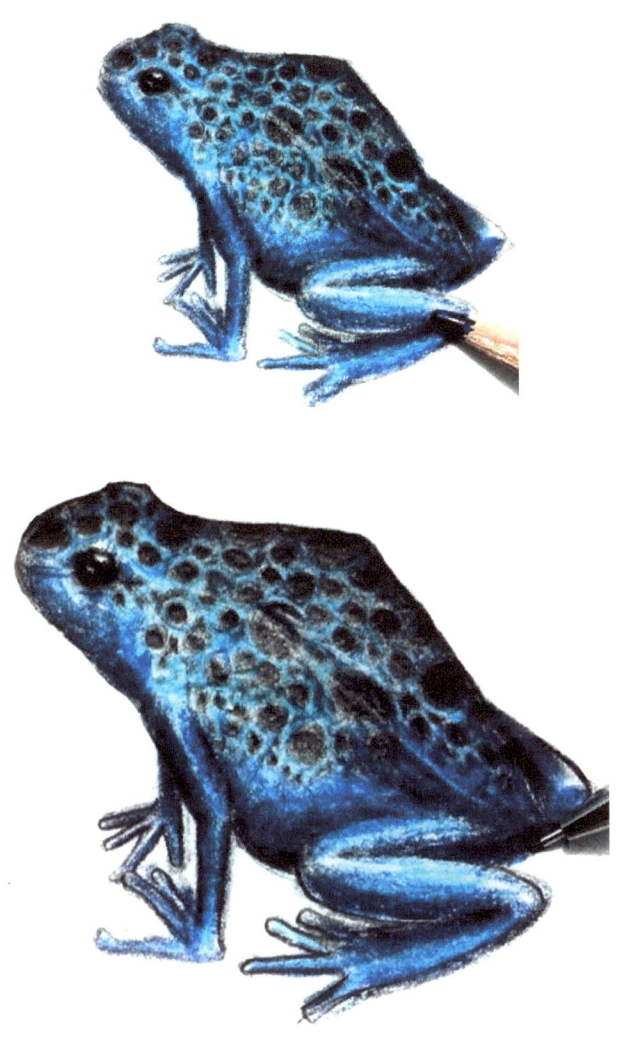

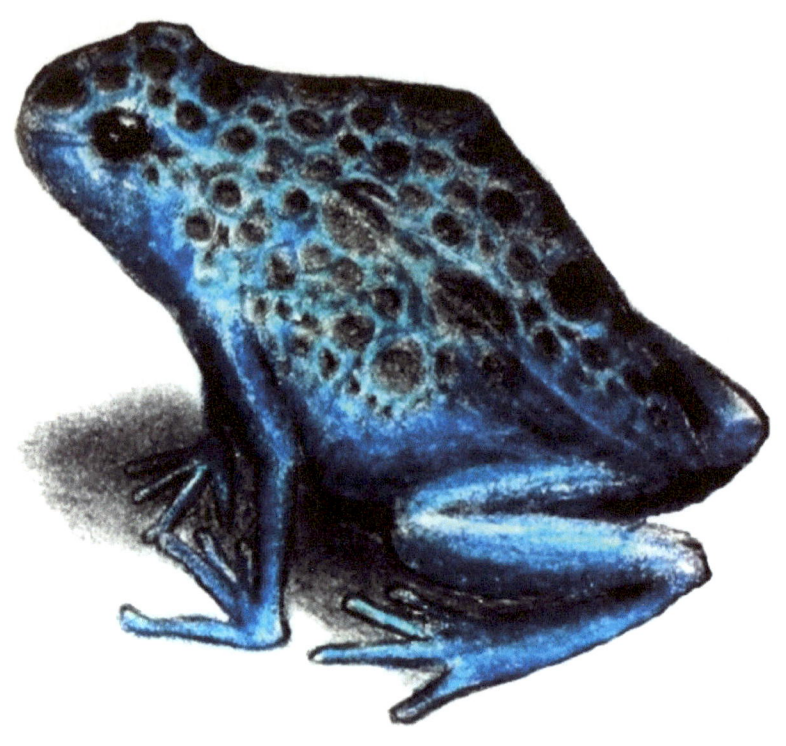

*Thank you for reading!*

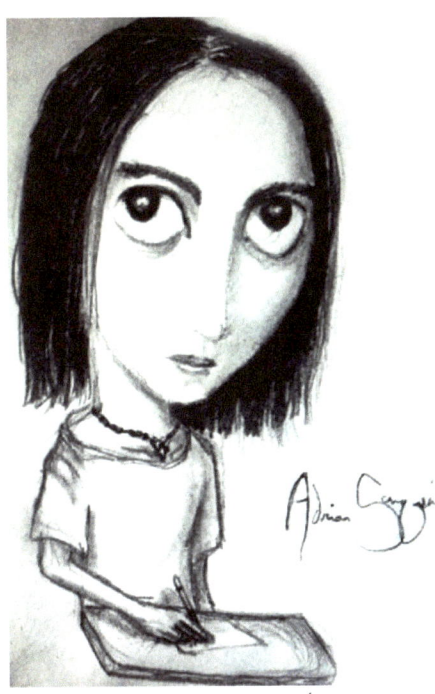

## Author Bio

**Adrian Sanqui**

Check out some of my other books:

*Manual Drawing for the Absolute Beginner*

*Learn to Draw People*

*Learn to Draw Cartoons*

*Learn to Draw Super Heroes*

*Learn to Draw Faces and Portraits*

*Learn to Draw Caricatures*

*Learn to Draw Animals in Pencil*

*How to Draw Lizards*

*Drawing Cartoon Animals for the Beginner*

*Drawing Insects for Beginners*

*Drawing Birds for Beginners*

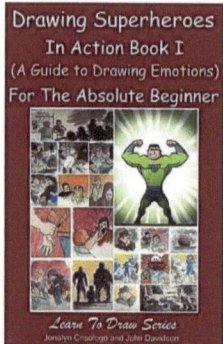

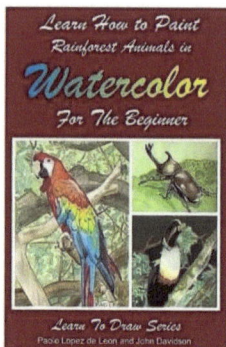

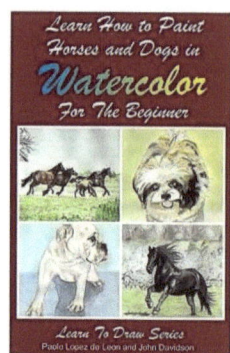

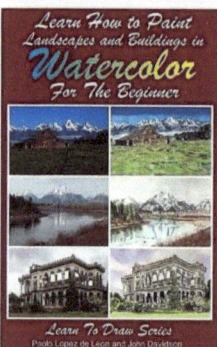

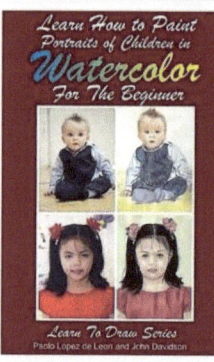

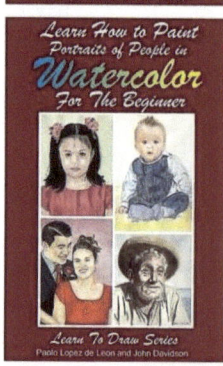

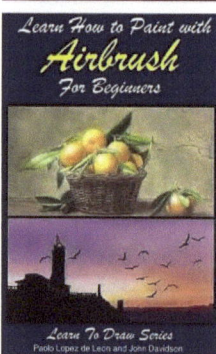

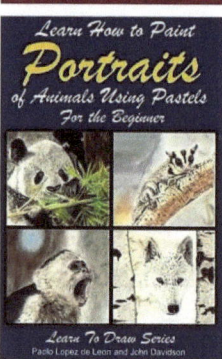

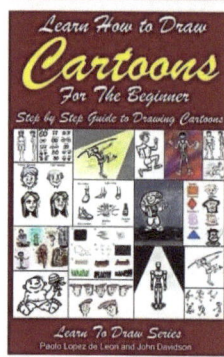

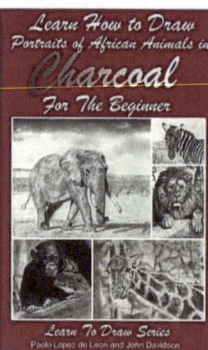

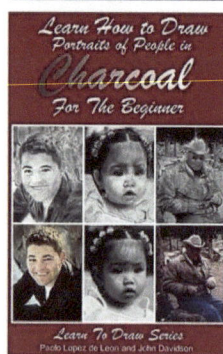

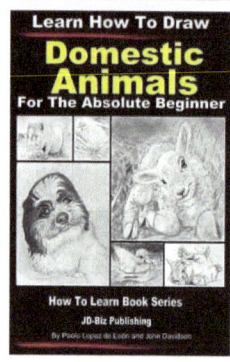

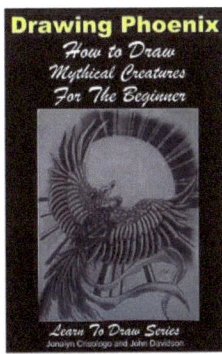

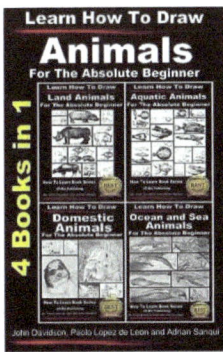

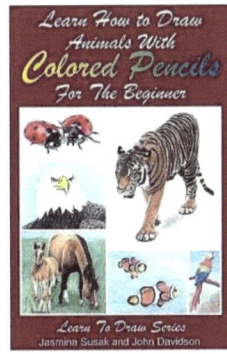

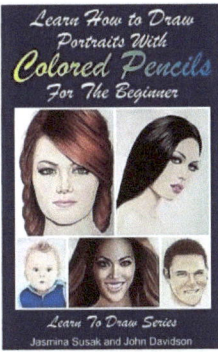

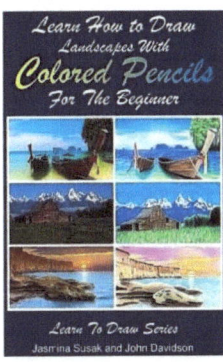

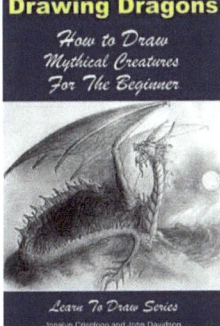

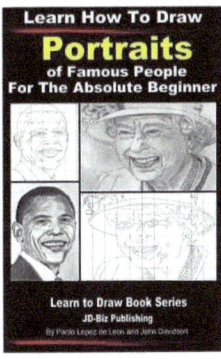

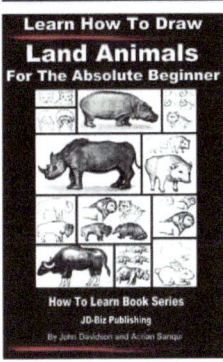

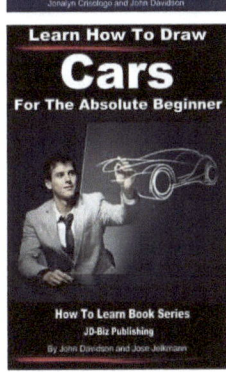

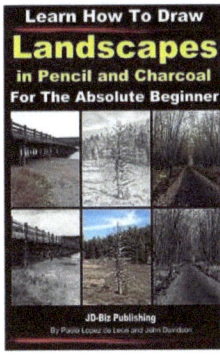

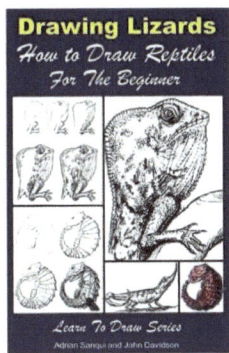

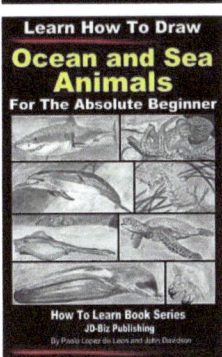

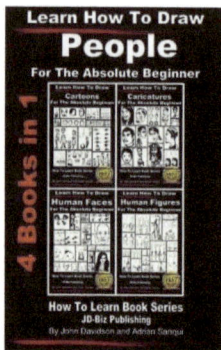

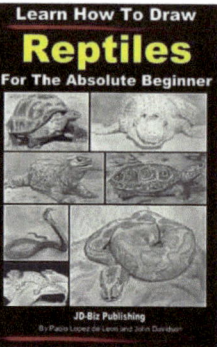

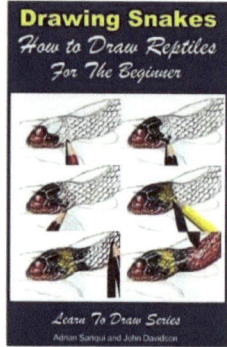

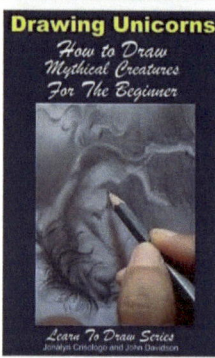

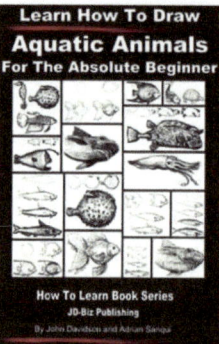

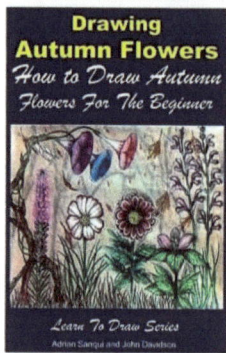

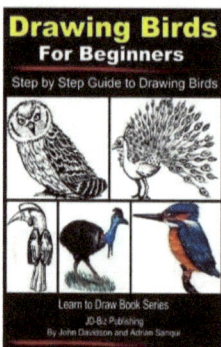

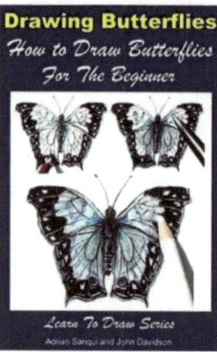

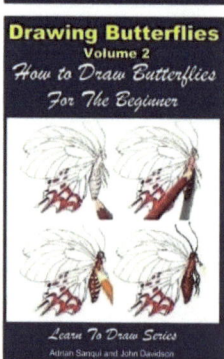

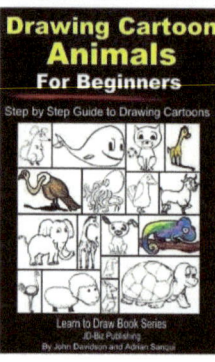

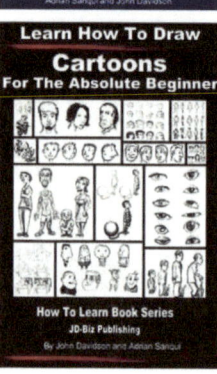

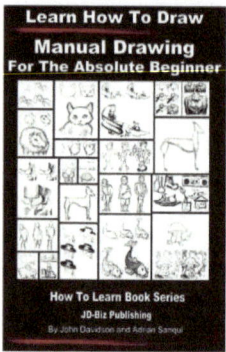

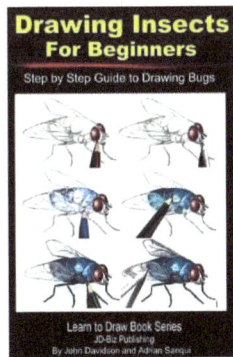

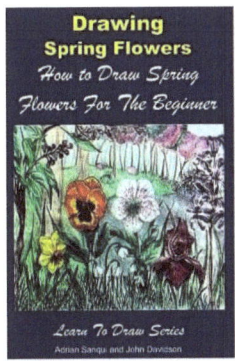

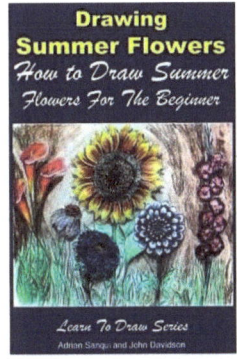

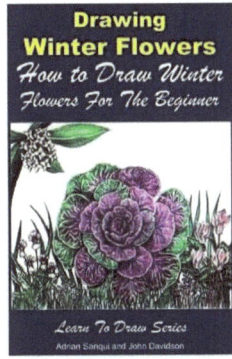

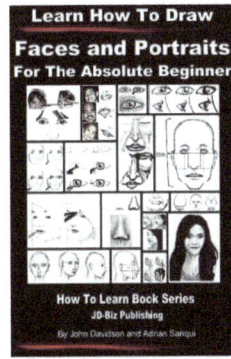

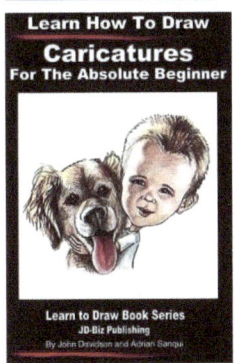

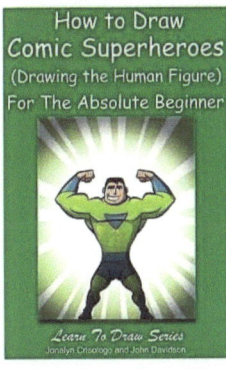

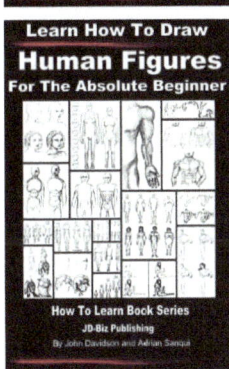

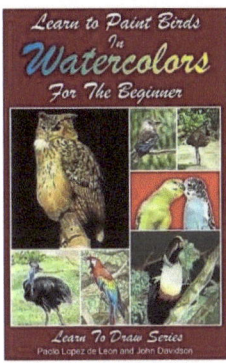

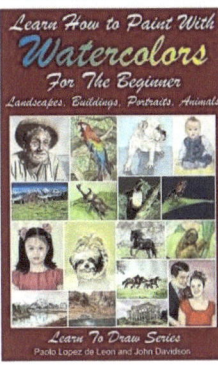

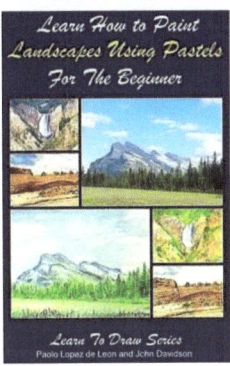

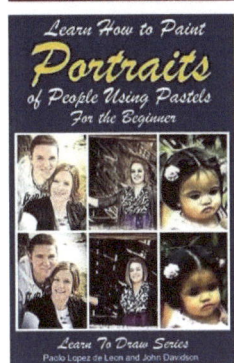

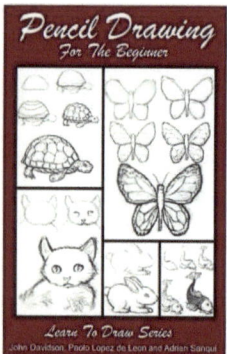

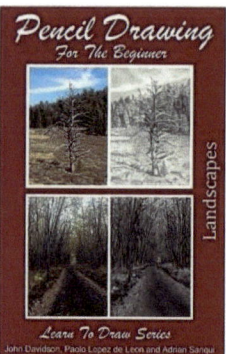

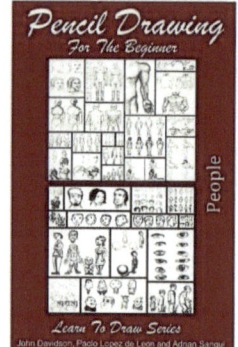

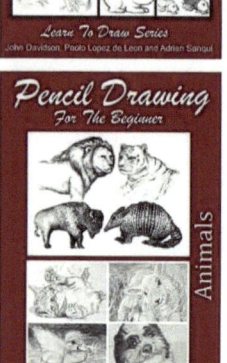

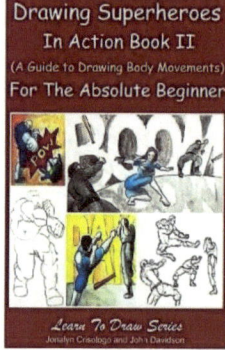

# Publisher

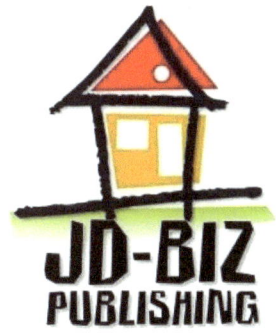

**JD-Biz Corp**

**P O Box 374**

**Mendon, Utah 84325**

http://www.jd-biz.com/

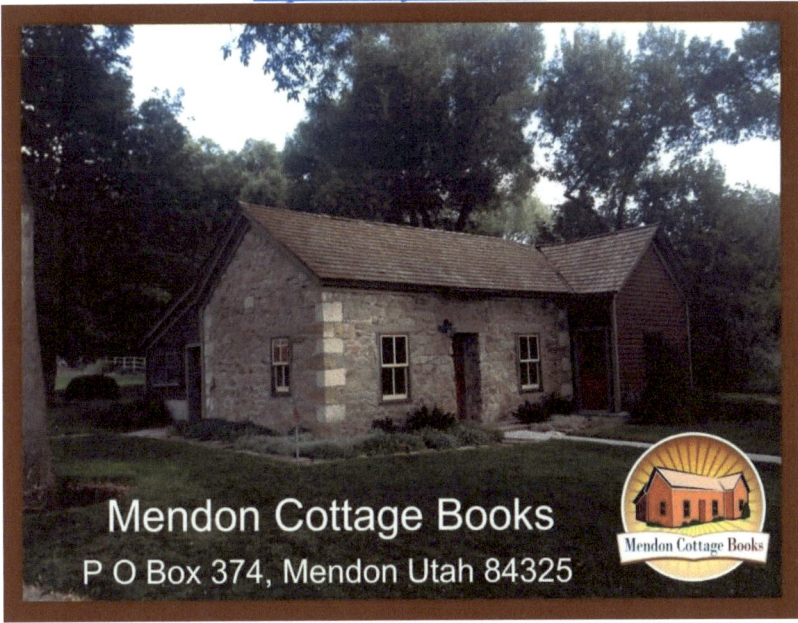

www.ingramcontent.com/pod-product-compliance
Lightning Source LLC
Chambersburg PA
CBHW040858180526
45159CB00001B/461